Love Pearls

Guidance for living a lifestyle of wholeness and Personal Freedom.

Series 1

Relationship Experts & Co-Authors
Love Jordan & D. Truth Jordan

Love Pearls
Series 1

TruLuv Experience
8550 W. Desert Inn, Suite 102-555
Las Vegas, NV. 89117

Cover Design and Illustrations: London Howard Photography

Editing: Avery L. Penn Sr.

23 Limited Editions copies printed in Peru.

Add Value to someone

else's life

Today!

(Karma Pays 100 Fold!)

~Truth~

TABLE OF CONTENTS

DEDICATION

With tireless Love to our children… We encourage you - to open your minds and believe! Your journeys are just beginning.

With humility, grace, and thanksgiving - To our parents and grandparents…

Your sage timing, eternal contributions and subtle guidance has flawlessly prepared us for all the "What's Next" moments that have placed us upon the pathway towards this; our own hallowed, gratifying journey!

We salute you!

You provided us exactly what we needed to overcome Life's adversities while reaching for and achieving our own personal greatness!

To our future generations…. The world is in your hands, cradle it with Truth and nurture it with Love.

FOREWORD
By Author Cynthia Walker

We are trained to invest in others, to support their visions and to encourage them.

We are trained to invest in stocks and bonds to make ourselves financially comfortable in the future.

For some reason it is rare that we are taught to invest in ourselves. We are our most important asset, we are a vision, and we need to be mentally sustained for our latter years.

Most times than not, we don't realize that we are broken or our treasure chest is empty, until it is.

At that moment we begin this scramble to figure out how to put the puzzle back together.

Or we try to find things to fill our empty treasure chest
and we begin a new journey to a new brokenness.

How do you change your path?

Stop training yourself to cry about it! (Spoiler alert)
Relationship experts Love Jordan and D. Truth Jordan
have created this instructional journey to get us to a place
of healing where the burdens of our past will finally be a
non-factor.

They teach us how to become one with the universe, to
have that unexplainable peace that we all desire. When
we are bound by our past we can't soar into our future. I
encourage you to read this book with an expectation that
when you reach the final page your life will be changed
forever because I know mine has.........

~*Cynthia Walker*

Love Embrace
(Affirmation)

I flow in *gratitude*

and appreciation for the

journey, as well as for those –

whom I am blessed – to be able

to share it with!

~Love~

Embrace the Truth

Success and Failure!

(Discipline and Resilience)

~Truth~

(1)

*Impoverished Mind

Deciding to shift from an impoverished mind-set after spending an entire life enslaved, undoubtedly can be one of the most challenging of all processes to navigate in life.

Impoverished Mindset: *Ingrained internal "knowledge" that keeps you believing - you don't have what it takes, and aren't good enough to WIN in life.*

Don't cringe if this is you.

You're in quiet company with millions of other impoverished minds throughout the world. Each seemingly wandering in search of answers that will aid in overcoming personal challenges.

They too are finding it challenging to create the lifestyle of "Personal Freedom" which they so deeply desire.

Just such an identical realization had dawned upon me, (that I too was part of that massive number of wanderers searching for my own virtuous path toward both spiritual and personal success) after once again, I was left with less than favorable results on another project I had taken on.

From my recollection, the story looked a lot like this:

Truth and I had been working on a project for what felt like a lifetime, when I decided to consult the Oracle deck.

The answers to the questions that I was asking, would be helpful in my gaining much needed insight into the area and direction in which we were traveling.

The one card that really drew my attention fell on the last day of a 7-day spread. *(This just means I drew 7 cards and turned one card over each day to receive guidance for each day of that seven-day period)*

In all its beauty, the card read

"Hidden Treasures".

However; it was upside down, which meant something entirely different from a projection of walking into a new cycle of abundance.

What awaited me instead was a beautiful message, pointing me towards the answer as to why my abundance was NOT flowing as initially visualized.

The fateful message revealed a lack of proactive actions on my part.
I dropped the ball, failing to ensure

that paramount milestones leading to the achievement of my goals were effectively checked off.

Instead of meeting gleeful success, my self-review pointed to a distinct discovery which bore a lack of personal discipline, a truncated level of self-confidence, and an inadequate sense of personal follow through.

I had no one, other than myself, to whom I could point the finger at for my nil results.

Stirred, yet not shaken by the saving denotations of this blessed *Love Pearl*, I readily put my ego aside (… *and believe me it wanted desperately - to come out swinging*) and I sat thankfully in the sensational clarity of my new-found awareness.

The Universe, with binding simplicity, was guiding me in saying, "YOU ARE the one that holds the key to your own freedom!"

And, my previous reasons for remaining in a place of wanting, of never truly being able to attain a lifestyle of personal freedom, were simply results of my embracing an impoverished mindset.

It had very little, if anything at all, to do with any kind of physical incapability.

I could hear the universe outwardly scolding me, screaming inwardly;

"Simply showing up at this stage of the game is no longer good enough".

I was being tasked with putting my thoughts, dreams, prayers, and desires into an active motion, if I were ever to experience the life of harmony, prosperity, abundance, and freedom that I had always envisioned.

The Universal law of Action - in its simplest definition states: In order for me to manifest things that I truly want in life, I must engage in the specific actions that support my thoughts, dreams, emotions, and words".

This Universal Law was absolutely going to take some time, patience, and practice to win over and fully master.

Does my story sound anything like yours?

Okay, maybe not the part about the Oracle card reading. (LOL).

I realize that not everyone embraces guidance in this fashion. But, I have to say for us, this divination adds value when incorporated properly.

However; back to my original thought; because I could go on and on sharing all the wonderful things about all the resources that are available to us when seeking guidance from the universe.

So, can you identify with your own lack of actions, a waning self-confidence or self-discipline?
Have you noticed an inadequacy in following through with requirements necessary to achieve your own initially stated goals?

A root cause of this dis-ease stems from being creatures of habit in our daily thoughts and behaviors. These are learned traits which are passed down to each one of us via years of experiences which no longer serve us very well.

Which means, you have the power to change any current habits, thoughts and behaviors that produce nil results for you.

Start by using conscious actions and words of encouragement that support a life of wellness.

Now is the opportune time to fully embrace a more flowing environment that is supportive of your personal vision. One which will move you diligently into your own process of nurturing "Self" more fluently.

*Loving Action

To make your process of nurturing "Self" become more fluent, begin shifting gently into an Empowered Mindset today by taking Loving Action.

Trust yourself

Trust your inner guidance. It is your best friend in life.

Our higher self supports our vision of greatness by stepping in to support whenever it's in the best interest of our highest good.

Allow that intelligence to become the trusted beacon of your guiding force.

Allow for creativity, passion, innovation, motivation and inspiration to flow through you, and Trust that you got this.

Don't give up Re-evaluate:

No one has ever won a race by not finishing it.

Even at the most brutal of places, on the many path's you'll travel, DON'T GIVE UP!

Those places along the way...extract from them what you must and build your character, resilience, drive, and motivation to catapult you into a "Freedom" Mind-set.

To help you move through the resistance more lovingly, simply reevaluate your plans.

Often, all that needs to happen to get you heading north is for you to go back and fine tune what you've already designed.

No need to reinvent the wheel.

Explore ways in which you can find a new approach at achieving an old dream.

Magic can be made when we allow our vision to evolve and transform completely.

Disengage

"Not all people, places, and things are in your best interest."

Growing up, my mother was very

particular about the group of friends my siblings and I hung out with.

She would say, "Not all people, places, and things are in your best interest."

Have you ever watched or read a biography on a highly-successful person?

Ask yourself, do they surround themselves with people who are in alignment with the direction of their success?

Or, do they lug around hindrances and unmotivated lackeys who do nothing other than tend to drag them down?

Choose your Tribe wisely throughout the course of your life.

You only have to turn on the television to witness the many folks who deviate from their path - following lost causes, only to find themselves going down the road of struggle, pain and strife - instead of the one which openly invites achievement, joy, and completely fulfilled success.

Remember, even in personal associations, we are still only as strong as our weakest link!

Change your thoughts.

We are our own worst critic.

BUT WAIT!!! There's great news ahead! You can learn to treat yourself royally simply by changing what information you allow to continually be broadcasting inside your head.

This is one sure-fire way for you to immediately become your number one admirer.

Admire all of who you are. If you need practice - stand in the mirror for one minute each day and speak positively about yourself - to yourself, until it becomes your continued internal dialog.

For us to manifest ultimate, lasting success in bringing our vision into reality, we must 1st become our own number one fan.

Keep your word.

Be that person - who can always be counted on to always operate at the pinnacle of the highest level of integrity and "forever - ever" … keep your word. If you commit, show up, and always be fully present in that which you've given your word to do.

It feels amazing; when we can "Show up"... and "Show out!!!

Now, I'M sure you're wondering if I was ultimately successful at shifting away from my former Impoverished Mindset....and all I have to say is, "you're reading my breakthrough.

The proof that these gentle approaches to growing, healing, and expanding actually do work.

Take - Action!

"If you do what you've always

done, you'll get what you've always

gotten."

~ Tony Robbins~

****** *Activity Page* ******

Make a list of "Empowered Mindset" Loving Actions to incorporate into your new daily routine.

Love Embrace
(Affirmation)

I Lovingly Embrace the infinite
opportunities before me,
so that I may create the most
beautiful physical
representation from my
intentions and actions..

~Love~

Free Your Self…

Start with your mind!

(And your body will follow!)

~Truth~

(2)

*Letting Go of Anything

We can all use guidance every now and again, so I'm not the first to admit it.

Over the years, as a grand gesture, I've enlisted the services of a few helpful professionals.

I've done this, when needed to gain perspective along with positive control over my life.

I sought out one particular counselor via referral from my insurance company…

He allowed for our sessions to become a Safe Haven for me to just sulk - for most or all 50 – minutes of our meeting each week.

Most days, he would sit silently, relaxed in the comfort of his therapist's chair - just glaring at me; as if he were watching the formation of a magical horn which grew languidly from the middle of my forehead.

But, I didn't care.

In theory, the only one I needed to show up for me, was me.

The therapist was getting paid regardless of my state of being.

So, my naive attitude was... "What did his advice have to do with my healing?"

Nevertheless, on one occasion, while I was knee-deep in my emotions, and I felt as if I were bleeding tears from my heart, without warning he yelled sternly...

"STOP CRYING"!!!

"Why - are you always…CRY-ING?"

Struck instantly speechless, by the sudden severity of his tone, a wave of all-encompassing shame, embarrassment, and then, anger - rushed up, then in, and all throughout me; in just a matter of a very few minutes.

I went mum… It was the helpless, chastised feeling that a child who'd just been caught stealing treats from a candy store must register upon realizing – that THE JIG WAS UP!

And… In that moment, I knew plainly just what my therapist had noticed as well; and that was - that I had nowhere else to go - but in.

I too asked myself… silently, "Why - are you crying?"

Opening my mouth to attempt to formulate a reply, I realized that… I couldn't. I had NOTHING! No words to provide the man an answer.

I didn't know.... I really had no idea why it was that I was crying.

My first thought was, "this is what you're "supposed" to do in therapy, right??? Or so I thought???

Then a realization suddenly hit me, that the only relief that I had been able to find through therapy, was in the trusted safety of being able to allow my heart to bleed tears over my woes during our weekly session's.

Which then began to unleash a tsunami of a thousand spigots, which once again, turned the tears back on.

Starring compassionately into my eyes, like only a true - friend would, when trying deeply to connect to the very cerebral basis of your core, to save you from any additional sorrow or heartache...

He leaned forward and said, in a quite matter - of -fact manner…

"If you're ever going to heal, you're
going to have to
LET THAT SHIT GO."

~Anonymous Therapist~

***Lesson**

LETTING GO of all that we think we know, all the ways in which we were programmed.

Letting go of ego, self-identity, of guilt, pain, fear, blame, and judgment.

Letting go of old materials, clutter, unhealthy habits, grievances, burnt out relationships, and ALL of the THINGS that smell of bondage to past pain.

It's mandatory to release yourself, if you're ever going to flow in life, and become whole in total physical and spiritual wellness. There just ain't no other way. You're going to have to Let That SHIT GO!!!!

*Loving Action

Acceptance

We can't change the past. Anything that has already happened - is final.

So, we must begin the journey of letting go; by first accepting things for what they actually are. Even if you're not satisfied with the endmost result.

What's done is done.

"Forgiveness is an attribute of the strong".

~Mahatma Ghandi~

Forgiveness

Have you heard the phrase, "Forgiveness is for you"?

Well that's correct. Forgiveness is always for you even when it doesn't feel that way.

The alternatives to not forgiving, and not letting go, look a lot like

- stress, high blood pressure,
- loss of hair,
- appetite fluctuations,

- weight gain and/or loss,

waste of valuable resources such as time, energy, even money in many scenarios, and many more undesirable side effects that keep you living in a cycle of insanity.

Do I really have to spell it out even more?

- Has a negative impact on mental health,
- Creates distance between you and those you love,
- Leaves negative impressions on your children

You get the point right?

The most effective way I've found to navigate forgiveness, is by finding the blessings inside the lessons.

What does that mean exactly? That means identifying what lesson blossomed from the situation after the storm cleared.

What value were you able to capture from the experience?

Shift into a state of awareness so that you're able to identify your Lessons & Blessings.

Doing so will more lovingly aid your process in letting go, and opening the door to Forgiveness.

Forgiving yourself first, and eventually extending the olive branches to others, because you'll realize just how valuable forgiveness truly is for your entire well-being.

There's no time like the present, let's begin now!

****** *Activity Page* ******

*List Page

Month______Day_____Year_____Time______

(Bring into awareness 5 Lessons that've added value on your journey by way of Forgiveness.)

1

2

3

4

5

*List Page

Month______Day_____Year_____Time_____

(Now, list 5 things that need your attention, and begin forgiving today.)

1

2

3

4

5

Spirit Writing

Equally powerful for learning the art of letting go, is utilizing the practice of Spirit Writing.

Writing out our feelings and emotions is an essential way for us to effectively work through, and process more lovingly letting go.

Embrace Spirit writing

Sit in a place that provides you with the level of privacy and security you need to write uninterrupted.

Choose a location that allows you to write from a place of nonresistance and love for yourself.

Begin this journey by writing all that you are feeling, sensing, and experiencing in the moment.

Spirit Writing should be incorporated into your daily, weekly, or monthly routine.

***Spirit Writing**

Month______Day_____Year_____Time_____

I feel...

Declutter

Most wouldn't think holding on to old stuff such as clothing, and household goods that no longer work, as being the clutter that creates additional problems for us in our daily life. But it does!! It is a FACT!!

How you keep the space(s) in your physical world is a direct reflection of what your internal world is looking like.

When you observe your space(s) do you feel:

A. Empowered?

B. In control?

C. Confident?

D. Secure?

E. Healthy?

F. Courageous?

G. Free?

H. Light?

A	B	C	D	E	F	G	H		
								Mo________Day____	
								Yr______Time____	
								Mo________Day____	
								Yr______Time____	

(Provided are 2 opportunities to track your emotional state.)

Or, do you feel:

1. Bogged down?

2. Drained?

3. Overwhelmed?

4. Pained?

5. Depressed?

6. Restless?

7. Irritable?

8. Unfocused?

1 2 3 4 5 6 7 8

Mo_______ Day___

Yr_____ Time____

Mo_______ Day___

Yr_____ Time____

(Provided are 2 opportunities to track your emotional state.)

If you feel the latter of the two observing list, you're in a place where Letting Go is essential for Self-Well-being.

Embrace decluttering now by making an awareness of your external spaces.

Do this by creating a list of every space in your physical world that need's a good spring cleaning.

Commit to cleaning them out one at
a time, and create a recurring
calendar reminder for yourself to
aid in consistency.

Make a life changing habit of
Letting Go of anything that no
longer serves your highest purpose
today.

*Space Cleaning List

Month______Day_____Year_____Time_____.

Spaces to Clear

Love Embrace

Letting Go is growth being Experienced.

It is the full Essence of the Expression.

Embrace Evolution for the prize is Healing.

~Love~

Everything In This World is

meant to be impermanent.

(Let go of the old frequently....

Keep your space clear...and Experience

the results you envision.)

~Truth~

(3)

*Taking Time for Me

It's truly fascinating…….

People begin appearing on the beach every evening from seemingly out of nowhere in Huanchaco, Peru.

I learned, they come to bask in the magnificent energy of TrueLove. Experienced through the energetic shift from one state of being, to the next.

As I stood, gazing along with everyone else, at the gigantic fireball floating above Mother Ocean on this extraordinary evening, my flesh began to still.

I then felt love flow in, up, through and around me - leaving loving tingles in her wake.

Hearing ever – so – clearly, My senses began to become in-tune with the soft, almost inaudible sounds of Angels and the melodically sweet Sister Wind singing prayers of gratitude, love, appreciation and thanks to the Universe for Divine magnificence.

And... as I wistfully began to feel my inner chi become caught up in the flow of Universal love, oneness and consciousness, I chimed in.

Offering up my prayers of gratitude for the journey I've been blessed to experience, learn, grow, and heal by. Inhaling deeply with purpose and gratitude...

I then exhaled, surrendering my undivided attention to the space that was created, to take time for me.

***Lesson**

The precious time we take for self allows for our body's rejuvenation and repair.

It's not always easy with such busy lives, but you can make it happen. And once you do you'll find how easy it actually can be to take time for self.

Time for self can and should be incorporated into our daily schedules.

***Loving Action**

Walking

Incorporate slow meditative walks into your mornings, lunch hour, or after dinner meals.

By walking mindfully, one has the ability to slow down, pay closer attention to their thoughts, and set intentions that are in alignment with their highest good.

This is a beautiful step in the direction of wellness.

Get out in nature

Nature is our playground. Venture out and take a breath. No excuses! It takes only a few moments to claim wellness every day. Incorporate some much needed one on one time with self.

Embark on a new hobby.

Expand in growing a talent or skill.

Higher educational classes, and self-empowering workshops are bold, loving approaches to re-engaging in your life. As well as an opportunity to share your loving, creative energy in a way "only you" can.

Turn off the cell phone.

Believe it or not, sometimes we have to disconnect from our devices.

Steal those much needed moments
back and take time for self.

If it's important, they'll call back!

Relax.

I like to cuddle up with a nice warm

non-alcohol beverage, inhale deeply
and watch the stars sparkle.

Can you feel the Exhale and
Relaxation just thinking about it?

Meditate!

Take the first 15 minutes to Meditate upon rising, setting the tone for the day.

It's Life Changing!

Nothing says "I love me" like spending dedicated time with self, and taking a breath to expand in conscious awareness.

Get creative! Make a list of "Taking Time for Me" Loving Actions you enjoy.

Loving Actions List

Love Embrace
(Affirmation)

I inhale deeply, with

purpose, and gratitude!

I give time and space my

undivided attention!

~Love~

Embrace the Truth

Live Your Dream Life

Right Now!

(Or)

Live the rest of your life dreaming!

~Truth~

About Love Jordan

- Love Jordan is a gifted healer & mystic, Spiritual teacher, Inspirational Speaker and Author, who's devoted her life to creating a loving bridge of Divine guidance, and healing to those seeking peace, understanding, a deeper connection and resolve in life.

- Love has been instrumental in assisting countless individuals, couples, families, and organizations in achieving a lifestyle of complete wellness and Personal Freedom.

- Love began healing at the ripe age of 22.

- Love teaches various healing and leadership methodologies that support individuals and organizations in expanding their spiritual, emotional, physical, and intellectual intelligence.

- Love is one of Americas Leading experts in Transformational Leadership, Personal Freedom, and in achieving a life of Authenticity and wholeness.

- Love is currently living in Huanchaco, Peru enjoying Personal Freedom and wholeness, obtained by way of the guidance she and her adoring husband share with all whom seek liberation.

About Truth Jordan

- Truth Jordan is a Spiritual Leader, philanthropist, mentor, and inspirational speaker. A loving and devoted husband and father, inspiring his family and countless others by his actions, and lifestyle of Personal Freedom.

- Truth is a decorated U.S. military-combat veteran. Retired by injuries

sustained in combat, Truth credits
meditation, forgiveness, and surrender
in conjunction with other mind-over-
matter techniques, to his mastery of
personal energy.

- Truth currently teaches "mastery of
personal energy" by helping others to
better understand human energy, and
the reactive responses of the mind
and body.

- Truth & Love are among the first
energy healers to offer Rieki in the
holistic Mecca of Peru. And, they are
the very first couple to perform
tandem Reiki "Energy Healings" in

Huanchaco, Peru - where their home is lovingly considered "The House of Healing" (La Casa de Curaciòn).

- Truth & Love have been healing spirits across the United States since early 2010.

Find More Love Pearls

www.truluvexp.com

Love Pearls

- *Impoverished Mind, Letting Go of Anything, Taking Time for Me*
- *Surrender, Awareness, No Regrets*
- *Relationships, Triggers, Egoism*

Relationship Love Pearls

- *Money in Relationships*
- *Co-Creating in the Kitchen*
- *Romantic & Non-Romantic Relationships*

TruLuv Children's Books

- *Liberty's Magic Tail*
- *Prince Benny & the Flu*
- *Special Wanders - Lost in Camelot Woods*